# THINGS
## TO DO
### NOW THAT YOU'RE
# 70

First published in Great Britain in 2025
by Hamlyn, an imprint of
Octopus Publishing Group Ltd
Carmelite House
50 Victoria Embankment
London EC4Y 0DZ
www.octopusbooks.co.uk

An Hachette UK Company
www.hachette.co.uk

The authorized representative in the
EEA is Hachette Ireland,
8 Castlecourt Centre,
Dublin 15, D15 XTP3, Ireland
(email: info@hbgi.ie)

Distributed in the US by
Hachette Book Group
1290 Avenue of the Americas
4th and 5th Floors
New York, NY 10104

Distributed in Canada by
Canadian Manda Group
664 Annette St.
Toronto, Ontario, Canada M6S 2C8

Graeme Kent asserts the moral right to
be identified as the author of this work.

ISBN 978-0-60063-877-3

A CIP catalogue record for this book is
available from the British Library.

Printed and bound in China

10 9 8 7 6 5 4 3 2 1

Publisher: Lucy Pessell
Designer: Dani Leigh & Isobel Platt
Senior Editor: Tim Leng
Assistant Editor: Samina Rahman
Production Manager: Peter Hunt

Picture Credits: iStock

# THINGS
# TO DO
## NOW THAT YOU'RE
# 70

hamlyn

# INTRODUCTION

In case you are wondering about your life, now that you've reached 70, here are some suggestions:

Why not run for president? Or go into space? Or why not perhaps try to win an acting Oscar?

(Like Joe Biden, William Shatner and Sir Anthony Hopkins respectively.)

Or reach a new level in your career, like Picasso, novelist P G Wodehouse, or film directors John Huston and Robert Altman?

Well, all the achievements listed above were performed after the age of 80 or 90. So don't jump the gun. And don't you dare give up on any of your ambitions. If you have been good at one thing all your life, you might well find you are even better at another. Starting from your level of experience and accomplishment is very different to someone who is starting from scratch.

In your seventies you can be incredibly active and fit, healthy and happy. And quite as much as engaged with life as those of any other age. There is hardly any sphere of life in which your perspective might not prove useful. You have so much energy and helpfulness to offer, and others (both younger or older) will benefit enormously from the encouragement, company, humour and solace you have to offer them. Now is the time to find new groups with whom to share enthusiasm, friendship and happiness.

(Before reaching an age where you start thinking about going into space, that is.)

**Give – make it a habit to be generous not just with money, but with your time and your energy.**

Make each grandchild feel special by having one special and particular day dedicated to each one. Plan an outing or activity to spoil your grandchild and yourself.

**Remember the great pleasure of being a grandparent – you get to hand the children back at the end of the day.**

If I had to live my life again, I would make a rule to read some poetry and listen to some music at least once a week; for perhaps the parts of my brain now atrophied would thus have been kept active through use.

CHARLES DARWIN

Respect any rules that your children have made for their children. Don't spoil your grandchildren (too much) or undermine your child's authority as a parent.

**Start putting together your own collection of children's bedtime stories – ones you have heard, read, or made up yourself.**

Relinquish family responsibilities with grace. The time will come, if it has not already, when your children will want to take over the planning of family get-togethers.

**Blessed are those who can laugh at themselves, for they shall never cease to be amused.**

ANONYMOUS

Be aware of the wisdom and experience of others, but only insofar as these will help you choose your own path.

**Reflect upon your recent actions and thoughts. Can you discern patterns in your actions and reactions to situations?**

Consider how your personality is projected to other people. If you were another person, would you like the current you?

As one grows older,
one climbs with
surprising strides.

GEORGE SAND

**Polish up on any talents that you have, or find new ones by taking up a new hobby.**

Preserve the youth of your mind by seeing if you can name three actors from one of the TV shows you loved in the 1960s. Test your friends!

## PRACTICE SAYING 'NO.'

DON'T WORRY
ABOUT STRESS.
YOU PROBABLY
EXPERIENCED PLENTY
OF THAT AT WORK
WHEN YOU WERE NOT
IN CHARGE OF WHAT
HAPPENED. NOW YOU
ARE IN COMMAND
OF YOUR LIFE.

Old age is like everything else. To make a success of it you've got to start young.

**FRED ASTAIRE**

**Find a neglected piece of land and reclaim it for a community project.**

REVISIT THE PLACE OF YOUR BIRTH.

Make a time capsule.
Spend time with your family
deciding what to include,
then package it securely
and bury it for someone
to dig up in the future.

Be selective with your new activities. Before long you will be so busy you will wonder how you ever found time to go to work.

**Most of us do our best work in the mornings. Shift more and more decision-making activities to before noon.**

Save money by going to the hairdresser or barber on senior citizens' days (but remember that you might find some people there who are actually old!)

When Time who
steals our years away
Shall steal our pleasures too,
The mem'ry of the past will stay,
And half our joys renew.

THOMAS MOORE

Embark upon a regime of swim training. Swimming exercises the muscles, lungs and heart. It also develops suppleness, strength and stamina without placing undue strain on the body.

## GO THE WHOLE HOG AND BECOME A GROUPIE ON A 'GOLDEN OLDIES' TOUR.

Get a medical check-up that assesses your pulse rate, cholesterol level, lung capacity, blood pressure, vision, and hearing. Do it every six months, even if you think there is nothing wrong with you.

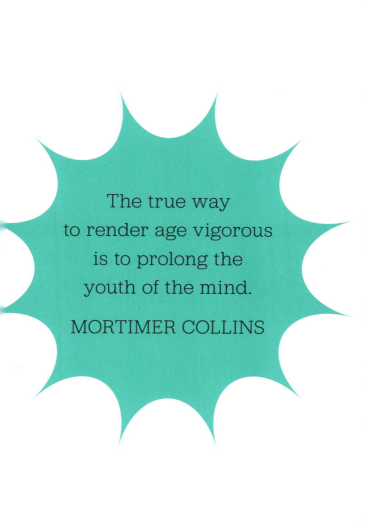

The true way
to render age vigorous
is to prolong the
youth of the mind.

MORTIMER COLLINS

Consider the advantages of tai chi, a series of exercises designed to combat stress and fatigue, improve flexibility, and encourage harmony between mind and body.

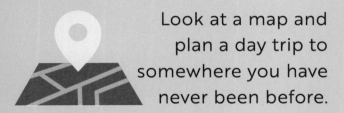

Look at a map and plan a day trip to somewhere you have never been before.

Take risks. Live a little. Strike up a conversation with a cute guy sitting next to you on public transport. You might come away with a new friend and an ego boost.

Glory in your age. In the 2004 San Diego Senior Olympics, one of the soccer teams called itself 'Vintage', while another, even more down-to-earth, entered as 'Old as Dirt'.

**Arrange to spend more time with people who love, cherish, and value you. That's not selfish – if they love you, they will be happy too.**

Keep mentally alert. Put aside time for crossword puzzles and games such as chess, bridge and Scrabble.

**TRACK DOWN A LONG-LOST FRIEND AND TALK OVER OLD TIMES.**

It's not the years in your life that count. It's the life in your years.

ABRAHAM LINCOLN

On 25 January, you can hold a Burns Night supper in memory of Scots poet Robert Burns. Eat haggis, recite the traditional 'Ode to a Haggis', drink single malt whisky, and enjoy the company of friends.

Consider the eight noble truths of Buddhism: right knowledge, right attitude, right speech, right action, right living, right effort, right mindfulness, and right composure.

**In any forward planning, always remember the great acronym S. K. I. – Spend the Kids' Inheritance.**

TAKE UP POTTERY. IT'S CREATIVE, FUN, AND CHALLENGING.

Learn a language. If you are keen to live abroad one day, you'll be delighted to be able to communicate with the locals. In any case, speaking another language is a useful skill to have and a fantastic excuse to go abroad on vacation.

Add a touch of glamour to your life. If you live near a film or television studio, become an extra in crowd scenes.

The pace of life is slower in the country. Decide whether you hanker after peace and quiet after a lifetime living in a vibrant city.

A good head and
a good heart are
always a formidable
combination.

**NELSON MANDELA**

**REMEMBER: YOU'RE ONLY PHYSICALLY YOUNG ONCE, BUT YOU CAN STAY MENTALLY YOUNG INDEFINITELY.**

Before you get any older, do something about training your memory. Forgetfulness is not inevitable, but you have to work at preventing it.

Take nothing at face value. At your age you can appreciate subtleties and nuances that you would once have missed.

Regard friendship
at 70 as a refuge.
"The bird a nest,
The spider a web,
Man friendship."

WILLIAM BLAKE

Learn to listen more to friends and family. "A bore is a person who talks when you want him to listen."

AMBROSE BIERCE

**Always show enthusiasm. Nothing is more attractive and people will constantly be drawn to you.**

Think – if you vanished tomorrow, what would you be missed for most? Those are the important things. The rest is just incidental.

Study ways to look after the planet. People will want to use it after you've finished with it.

LEARN TO KEEP YOUR TEMPER
IN ALL CIRCUMSTANCES. THERE
IS NOTHING SO IRRITATING
AS SOMEONE WHO CAN'T BE
PROVOKED INTO A ROW.

Pick something you've never
been able to do, like swimming,
for example, and learn to do it.
You'll be so proud of yourself for
having overcome your inability.

Make a list of five books you've
always intended to read but
never got around to. Give
yourself a certain amount of
time to get through each one.

Walking staves off heart
disease, reduces the risk
of high blood pressure,
improves muscle tone,
fights back pain, and
guards against respiratory
problems. Start gently
and build up to 30
minutes' walking a day.

**Buy a yo-yo and try to remember how to do all those tricks you could do as a kid.**

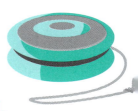

LEARN TO PLAY BRIDGE. IT'S SOCIABLE, COMPETITIVE, AND REQUIRES BRAINS RATHER THAN LUCK.

**Go to Egypt and visit the sights. Take the opportunity to ride a camel. It will probably be the worst riding experience you'll ever have but it's fun to say you've done it.**

Cherish your
friends – new and old.
"The friendship between
me and you I will not
compare to a chain,
for that rains might
rust, or the falling
tree might break."

WILLIAM PENN

Be slow to
fall into friendship,
but when thou art
in, continue firm
and constant.

**SOCRATES**

When you win,
make a point of being
magnanimous.
You may not win
every time.

**Why not take a course
in first aid? You never know
when you're going to need it.**

Make a list of all those irritating
jobs you should have done
around the house but never quite
got around to. Make a resolution
to do at least one of them each
week until they are all finished.

## BECOME A BLOOD DONOR. IT'S NOT EVERY DAY YOU GET THE CHANCE TO SAVE SOMEONE'S LIFE.

Dig a pond in your backyard and stock it with goldfish. They are much more interesting than people think and there is something very calming about sitting and watching them swim.

Spend a little time each day doing gentle bending and stretching exercises. It's good to stay supple as you get older.

It is a sweet thing,
friendship,
a dear balm
A happy and
auspicious bird of calm.

PERCY BYSSHE
SHELLEY

Don't ignore stress – it won't just go away. Always find ways to relax and lessen your stress levels.

**Buy a breadmaker and bake your own bread. It's tasty, nutritious, and you don't have to worry about all the salt and additives in commercially made bread.**

In the summer, when soft fruit is plentiful, make your own preserves. It isn't much trouble to do and they taste ten times better than the ones you buy.

Think seriously about
the ways in which
you wish to spend
your retirement.
Most people when
questioned want
to spend this time
engaged in meaningful,
useful activities,
not relaxing.

# CULTIVATE PATIENCE BECAUSE IT IS PART OF THE WISDOM THAT COMES WITH AGE.

Have an outfit tailor-made for you. We are all so used to off-the-rack clothes that we forget the sheer luxury of having something made.

Walking at least ten thousand paces each day will help you stay fit. It sounds like a lot, but you'll discover that it's nowhere near as difficult as you think.

Men seek out retreats
for themselves in the
country, by the seaside,
on the mountains...But all
this is unphilosophical
to the last degree...when
thou canst at a moment's
notice retire into thyself.

MARCUS AURELIUS

Pick some poems you love and learn them by heart. As you get older, the memory becomes a little less reliable unless you take the trouble to train it.

**Have you always wanted to write a book? If so, make this the year that you finally set pen to paper. Decide that this time you really are going to do it.**

Brew your own ginger beer. It's spicy, delicious, and because it has no alcohol, the whole family can enjoy it.

There are glimpses of heaven to us in every act, or thought, or word that raises us above ourselves.

ARTHUR P STANLEY

MAKE A RETURN VISIT TO
YOUR OLD SCHOOL. SEE IF
YOU CAN FIND YOUR INITIALS
CARVED ON A DESK.

Try building a ship
in a bottle. It's not that
hard when you know the
trick (you can find the
instructions on the Internet).

Try dowsing (you can find
instructions on the Internet).
It's an amazing experience
when the dowsing rods go
crazy in your hands.

Do not go where
the path may lead,
go instead where
there is no path
and leave a trail.

**RALPH WALDO
EMERSON**

Do things that bring you into contact with younger people. You can be of help to them, and their energy and enthusiasm will help you to stay young.

## WALK BAREFOOT IN THE PARK WITH YOUR PARTNER.

SPOIL GRANDCHILDREN BUT NOT SO MUCH THAT THEIR PARENTS GET ANNOYED.

Help your children by shouldering your share of the plethora of unpaid tasks for grandparents. According to a survey carried out in 2004, 49 percent of grandparents babysat regularly and more than 25 percent help with gardening and household repairs.

There are a lot of interesting people out there. Try to meet some of them, for example by joining a local club. Dr Samuel Johnson said, "Sir, I look upon every day to be lost, in which I do not make a new acquaintance."

Write your biography. It doesn't need to be published but it will 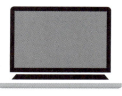 be instructive for you and interesting for your descendants.

Do your bit for the planet: make a rigorous inventory of all the things in your house that could be made environmentally friendly, whether it's appliances, insulation, or low-energy light bulbs: after all, they will also save you money!

AS YOU GROW OLDER, TRY HARD TO GROW WISER. THIS DOESN'T HAPPEN AS A MATTER OF COURSE; YOU NEED TO WORK AT IT.

Swimming with dolphins has become a bit of a cliché but if you haven't done it, you should certainly give it a try.

# WORK LONG AND HARD AT YOUR LOVE AND IT WILL WORK FOR YOU.

Weather the bad times – a period of transition can put some strain on even the steadiest of partnerships. The closer the bond you have, the better your chance of weathering any stress.

All the knowledge I possess
everyone else can acquire,
but my heart is all my own.

JOHANN WOLFGANG
VON GOETHE

**Introduce your partner to some of your interests. Go to an art gallery or to see a play together.**

Tread warily.
When you and your partner retire, it can take some time to adjust when you are both at home full-time.

**Have a Jacuzzi installed in your home. If you can't quite afford it, at least try one in a health club.**

[There are] three questions to
ask before a period of change:
'What is going on?'
'Why is it going on?'
'What can I do about it?'

ANTHONY WEDGWOOD BENN

You are now at the age
at which you can put your
experience, thinking, and
reading to good use by
contemplating and refining
your philosophy of life.
Try to visit at least one
famous shrine in the world.
Enjoy its beauty and historical
associations, and spend some
time there in contemplation.

LEAVE NOTHING THAT IS IN YOUR HEART UNSAID. NO ONE WILL KNOW UNLESS YOU TELL THEM.

**Do eye exercises. You can find the instructions on the Internet. If you do them regularly, they can reduce your need for glasses.**

Put up a hammock in your garden. Sleeping in one takes a bit of getting used to (and you might fall out once or twice) but once you get the hang of it, you'll love it.

**Take a course of self-hypnosis. It is easy to learn and can help to boost your confidence and eliminate negative thought patterns.**

Face painting shouldn't be just for kids. In fact, adults often find it interesting as well as fun. Try it at your next party and experiment with new identities.

**HOW ABOUT HAVING A SCULPTOR CARVE YOUR LIKENESS? VANITY? NO, YOU OWE IT TO POSTERITY!**

**Keeping up appearances is one thing; keeping up your spirits is everything.**

**CHARLIE CHESTER**

Yet another idea for those who like something a bit different – apply some bindi body jewels. They are stuck on and can be removed easily.

Have a family photo taken wearing clothes from another era. You can rent the clothes from historical costumiers.

If you feel a bit slouchy as you get older, you could try walking around the house with a book balanced on your head. It worked for great-grandma!

When the time for thinking is over, the time for putting beliefs into action will have come. Take inspiration from the great leader Gandhi, who said, "My life is my message."

Think of something you have always wanted to say to someone you know but have never had the courage to. Say it!

Watch a big sporting event with your partner but, just for once, skip saying, "What's all the fuss about?"

**In midsummer, why not try going for a night walk where you end up greeting the morning sun?**

Don't worry if you think you don't have as much natural talent as others. The great Albert Einstein said that he was no genius, but that he possessed the essential qualities of curiosity, obsession, endurance, and self-criticism.

Get a letter published in a newspaper. Think of something that really gets you worked up and write about it to the press. For once, be determined to say what you think.

**THINK OF ONE PERSON YOU HAVE WRONGED, SEEK THEM OUT AND APOLOGISE SINCERELY.**

Go on an archaeological dig. They always need amateur volunteers to do the hard part and you might learn something really interesting.

Immature love says,
'I love you because
I need you.' Mature love says,
'I need you because
I love you.'

ERICH FROMM

**AGE GIVES YOU A CHOICE: YOU CAN LET IT MAKE YOU MELLOW OR YOU CAN LET IT ROT YOU THROUGH AND THROUGH.**

Don't constrict yourself with time limits. Just get on and do whatever it is that you want to do and enjoy it.

YOU ONLY LIVE ONCE, BUT GET YOUR ATTITUDE RIGHT AND ONCE WILL BE ENOUGH.

A Japanese study of people's
diet in their later years
indicated that the fittest
and healthiest subjects
were those who ate only
until they were about 80
percent full. Consider
adopting this as a maxim.

It takes two

to speak the truth –

one to speak,

and another to hear.

HENRY DAVID THOREAU

**ALWAYS SEARCH FOR NEW THINGS THAT INSPIRE YOU BOTH WITH ENTHUSIASM.**

Before you set off on vacation, make it a rule to study the culture of the area you are going to visit, as well as the geography.

Break down each ambition into component parts. Use a checklist as you achieve each section. If you want to fly a plane, join an airfield, or book your first lesson.

Leap out of bed,
rush to the window,
and yell,
"Good morning, world!"

**Celebrate change –
you can't stop it from
happening so you may
as well embrace it.**

MAKE YOUR PARTNER
LAUGH OUT LOUD AT
LEAST ONCE EACH DAY.

I never deny,
I never contradict,
I sometimes forget.

**BENJAMIN DISRAELI**

Learn a new word every day.
A large vocabulary will help you
speak and write with authority.

**If you're married, hold
a ceremony to renew
your marriage vows.**

ATTACK ALL OF YOUR
PLANS WITH CONFIDENCE
AND OPTIMISM.

Grow old
along with me!
The best is yet to be.

ROBERT BROWNING

Consider developing any skills you have. You now have time to become a better musician, improve your skiing ability, and so on.

**Don't be too proud to accept help if it is offered. Just because you're older, it doesn't always mean that you are wiser.**

Congratulate yourself constantly. Remind yourself of what you have achieved already and use this to spur you on to greater things.

Draw upon your own experiences and use them in your grand plan. The great American primitive artist, Anna 'Grandma' Moses, was in her seventies when she started painting, using memories of her farming background from the 1860s to produce such paintings as *Catching the Thanksgiving Turkey*. She painted on flat boards in her bedroom and developed an international reputation.

Be in control.
Ignore enforced reasons
for making a change.
It is your life and you
are in charge of it.

## TINKER TO YOUR HEART'S CONTENT.

**Find a silly habit or hobby that you and your partner can enjoy as a couple. Put on old records on a Sunday afternoon and dance like you are teenagers again, or take up pottery classes together.**

A successful marriage requires falling in love many times, always with the same person.

**MIGNON MCLAUGHLIN**

Love seems the swiftest,
but it is the slowest of all
growths. No man or woman
knows what perfect love is
until they have been married
a quarter of a century.

MARK TWAIN

Be extra nice to the most irritating person you know. Maybe your change of attitude will be reciprocated.

**Give some of your time to charity work. It's great to give money but even better to give a bit of yourself.**

Learn to meditate. It's not hard to do, will relieve your stress symptoms, and help every area of your life.

# IF YOU HAVE ONE GOOD IDEA, SPEND TIME PERFECTING IT.

DON'T LET A LACK OF QUALIFICATIONS PUT YOU OFF DOING ANYTHING.

Start your own 'Where are they now?' list. See if you can trace any heroes – or villains – of your youth.

If you are happy where you are, don't change. The great popular composer, Irving Berlin, never learned to play the piano properly, although he wrote thousands of tunes. When he approached what would be the retiring age for most people, he decided against taking piano lessons. "I figured that in the time it took me to learn I could have written a few songs and made myself some money," he commented.

TAKE THE WHOLE
FAMILY OUT FOR
A PICNIC.

Get everyone in the
family to write down all
the good things that have
ever happened to them.

**TELL YOUR KIDS A
FUNNY STORY YOU
HAVE NEVER TOLD
THEM BEFORE.**

Give your partner an
unexpected gift to
symbolize your pleasure
in your long marriage.
It could be a garland of
flowers, or something
similar, to represent
the binding tie.

Enjoy oysters and a glass of champagne together.

**KEEP A PHOTO OF YOUR LOVER WITH YOU AT ALL TIMES.**

Make a special effort to get along with your partner's best friend.

Show a cheerful face to the world, but do not be foolhardily cheerful. Borrowing from the words of the poet Rudyard Kipling, if you can keep your head while all about you are losing theirs, you probably don't appreciate the true facts of the situation. Temper optimism with common sense.

WHEN AT THE BEACH, HAVE A FAMILY SANDCASTLE COMPETITION.

**Smile and wave at people in other cars. See how many return your greeting.**

When it's your anniversary, don't go to a fancy restaurant. Take the trouble to cook something special.

Oliver Cromwell said: "I beseech you, in the bowels of Christ, think it possible you may be mistaken." Pause to consider whether you might be at fault whenever you fall out with those you love.

With some like-minded enthusiasts, hire a luxury car for a day and go for a champagne picnic at a beauty spot.

Finish Do-It-Yourself projects that you start. Few things are less romantic than a gaping hole in the wall.

**ALWAYS SHARE PROBLEMS BUT DON'T LET THEM TAKE OVER YOUR LIFE.**

The time has come
for me to get my kite
flying, stretch out in the
sun, kick off my shoes,
and speak my piece.

HARPO MARX

Do something really challenging together. Climb Everest? Make a lasagne from scratch? The choice is up to you. All that matters is that you share a real adventure.

**Hold hands!**
**Why should only young lovers get to do this?**

Admire and praise your partner's good points. With a bit of encouragement, even more good points might emerge.

TAKE TIME TO
REVIEW MEMORIES
OF YOUR YOUTH.
WITH MATURITY,
YOU WILL
UNDERSTAND
THINGS THAT YOU
MISSED THE FIRST
TIME AROUND.

They say that time changes things, but you actually have to change them yourself.

**ANDY WARHOL**

When a kind thought comes to you, say it out loud. When you think of a cutting remark, keep it to yourself.

**Spend a little time counting all the good qualities your lover has brought into your life.**

WISE PEOPLE KNOW WHAT THEY SHOULD DO NEXT. BUT ONLY BRAVE ONES DO IT.

## LEARN FROM OTHER PEOPLE'S MISTAKES.

Work on your tolerance levels. See how long you can go in a day without judging anyone.

**Stop yourself from telling the same anecdotes over and over again.**

Visualize what you want to do. Hold onto that vision and really think it through before proceeding.

We haven't the
faintest idea what life
is really all about. The
most you can do is live
it to the best of
your ability.

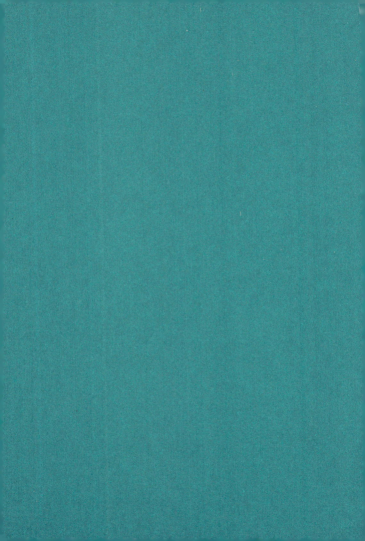